Slim

This book
belongs to:

Slim

A FANTASY MEMOIR

by
Cynthia Rowley

RIZZOLI
NEW YORK

Table of Contents

Rin-troduction

Just because your family isn't dysfunctional doesn't mean they're not crazy. Exhibit A: the Rowley clan. My kid brother used to make robot costumes out of recycled detergent bottles… *for a living.* My other brother was famous for running around the neighborhood backwards to better sculpt his calf muscles. Rather than giving us an allowance, my parents used to dare us to do stuff if we wanted extra money, as in "I'll give you two bucks if you kiss that fish head."

I love my family and had a near idyllic childhood growing up in a small town in the Midwest, but they can be a little nutty, present company included. I guess you could say this is a tribute to all their quirks, the ones I look back on fondly now, and the inklings of that creative spark leading me to a career in fashion. Like my clan back home, this collection is hard to define, part memoir, part fiction, part kid's book, and a chance to do some drawings.

I hope you enjoy it.

9

1

I wore them with a red petticoat and matching red ballet slippers.

Functional Fixedness

Pretty much, for all of junior high school, my mom was on a campaign against "functional fixedness," the notion that any object has but one single purpose. For this reason, she was not keen on store-bought toys or even fashion. The coloring books we had as children were nothing more than blank journals—her feeling being we weren't using our imaginations if the lines were already there. So I went to great lengths to reinvent the old junk collecting dust in our basement in the back of our closets and hanging in our garage. Most of the time my creations won praise from friends and family.

I turned the upstairs shower curtain into a sweet little dress, an umbrella into a kilt (pro: it's waterproof; con: bad luck to wear it inside), the silver ironing board cover into a reflector beach tote, and my old dollhouse furniture into earrings and hair accessories. I made a fall coat from my closet shoe organizer and a fluffy ski cap from all of the one-of-a-kind lost mittens we had lying around. For my first day back after Christmas break, I needed an extra special outfit, so I cut my dad's socks into strips and knitted them into legwarmers. That morning at school I had my first kiss from R. C. Treat. When my mom picked me up, I couldn't wait to tell her all about it. She seemed surprised, worried even.

"Where did he kiss you?!"

"On the playground."

"No, where on your body?"

"Twice, on the side of my head."

And that, ladies and gentlemen, was all the incentive I needed to keep going. The math in my head went something like this: more elaborate designs = better social life.

When the anniversary party for our next-door neighbors Steve and Taffy Hicks was over, how could I let all those helium balloons go to waste? Remembering the inflatable swimmies from when I was a baby, I put together a billowy dress with big net sleeves. Being extremely slight in stature, the minute those balloons cut loose, I was off—into the wild blue yonder. I think I fainted at the lofty old altitude of about ten feet so no one knows exactly how high or how long I was up there, but they found me in a supermarket parking lot a few towns away.

My parents nursed me back to health in my twin bed. While they did their best to make certain I had learned my lesson, I wondered if I could make it all the way to Manhattan.

"Oh yes, never again, I promise, Mommy."

At least not without putting rocks in my pockets ahead of time.

2

How to Turn Your Bathtub Into a Wishing Well

One time on a hot summer day, when I was babysitting myself at home, I decided to make some Kool-Aid. The problem was I couldn't reach the pitcher we mixed it in because my mom always kept it on the top shelf. No matter how many chairs I stacked together I just couldn't reach it. *Ah ha!* I thought. *I'll plug the bathroom sink and mix a batch right there!* I could dip my cup in like it was a porcelain punch bowl, kiddie moonshine. But, I have to admit, the last few cups did have sort of a "minty fresh" taste.

So when I set out to make my own wishing well a few weeks later, again it seemed like a natural solution to use the upstairs bathtub. I went about gathering materials: mud and stones from the driveway (not too much from one spot so as not to be detected), moss to cover the top edge of the tub, and a papier-mâché-covered Barbie that resembled the Statue of Liberty. After all, every good fountain has a statue.

Step One: Complete.

Step Two: Take all the change from dad's dresser. It wasn't quite enough so I resorted to stealing money from a baby (brother). Not everything in his piggy bank, but most of the silver.

Step Three: Lock the bathroom door.

Step Four: Fill the tub.

Step Five: Turn around. Make a wish. Aim. Release.

Too bad for me that my dad caught wind of my project soon after (ratted out by my bankrupted brother, no doubt). He stormed upstairs, rolled up his shirt-sleeves, dug through the muck, and ripped that plug right out of the tub. While I was being reprimanded and grounded for the next five years—"Young lady do you realize what kind of mess…"—an even big-ger calamity was brewing. All the mud and pebbles and blobs of green papier-mâché were running down the drain, clogging the plumbing for the whole house, including the sprinkler outside.

And with the blob went my good luck wishes. So much for playing the trumpet like Chuck Man-gione and having a body like Farrah Fawcett.

Now my only wish was that somehow I would live long enough to pay for this disaster by forfeiting my entire allowance for as long as I was "under their roof" and later garnishing my wages long into my future career as a Pan Am flight attendant.

As the discussion of my habitual objectionable character wore on and on behind the closed kitchen door, I heard a loud popping, then a sizzling sound coming from the family room. My dad heard it too and flung open the door to find a mini-fireworks display shooting out the back of our Magnavox TV as my little brother sat there and watched.

It turned out that after the piggy bank break-in he needed a safer place to stash his coins. The slits in the back of the television set looked exactly like a bank to him and thus his bad idea was born. So while I was grateful to him for diverting attention away from my foolishness, my alarm at the prospect of missing a month of Saturday morning cartoons dulled my appreciation down to zero.

Silently I blamed my dad for busting me first, because if the order had been reversed we would have had a concrete way to wish for a new TV. Oh, well. Oh, well.

"If only there was a badge for hair styling."

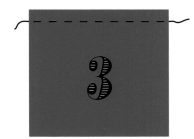

3

Badge Happy

I've always been a bit of an overachiever. Girl Scouts was no exception. As a Brownie I fantasized about the day I'd proudly don my green uniform, probably the same way minor league baseball players dream about trading up to the majors. But when I finally did become a Junior Girl Scout, I hated how drab the sash looked; it seemed so sad and vacant.

Immediately I went to work "decorating" it with merit badges. I think the first one I got was the cooking badge for my Baked Alaska and next came the camera badge, for which I had captured rare photos of the fabled Illinois brown squirrel in its natural habitat. For the music badge (geek alert), I learned to play reveille on the bugle. Needless to say, I was the toast of the annual jamboree.

I thought the more patches I had, the more seriously people would take me as the worldly fifth grader I longed to be. I could easily knock off two or three in a weekend, although technically my mom had to give the final sign-off. Forget about it. I was on Easy Street. She wasn't going to rat me out for a couple of petty requirements. She knew I could tie a sailor's knot if I just put my mind to it.

Guess again.

The more badges I got, the more of a stickler she became. Maybe she was afraid I'd zip through them all and have nothing to do the rest of the summer, or maybe she just didn't want to be seen as the first lady of pushover city.

I remember earning my sewing badge and fastening it to my sash with a safety pin instead of

"I think he even smiled for the camera."

stitching it on like the other ones. I figured once they've been duped into giving it to me, why continue conforming to their expectations? This was my punk rock rebellion against The Man (or in this case Mrs. Petersen, the Troop Leader). The real players in my troop had badges going all down the front and continuing up the back. Then you knew you'd arrived. I was a girl on a mission. I would not stop until I had petitioned the GSA to add new categories, because I'd bang out all the rest.

By the time seventh grade came along, I quickly became too embarrassed to wear my Girl Scout uniform to school on Wednesdays as was required. Girl Scouts was for little girls and I was fast approaching womanhood, or so I thought. Ironically, the thing I had given my all to in the hopes that classmates might see me as more mature eventually became an association that felt too babyish to pursue in earnest.

Psst…I still keep the sash on a hanger in my closet, ready to go at a moment's notice.

Swivel Hips

All I wanted in life was a trampoline. If I saved my babysitting money it would only take me about six years to buy my own. Unfortunately, I didn't have that kind of time. It was almost summer and I had to know my daredevil needs would be satisfied during those hot, lazy months.

They say that the first form of trampolining was performed by the Eskimos. Apparently, the boys would take turns tossing each other into the air on a walrus skin. So, really, how hard could it be to make one harnessing today's technology?

29

Steel pipe? Check.
Bungee cords? Check.
Canvas? Check.

We could build it from scratch!

The impulse to take matters into my own hands was not without precedent. When my brother and I were younger, we wanted a go-cart so badly but, of course, buying a new one was out of the question. Too flashy (read: expensive)! Only spoiled kids got things like that (read: those lucky ducks)! Easy enough to make a go-cart on your own, said my dad! And the feeling of pride we'd get from knowing we'd done it all by ourselves? Absolutely priceless!

The maiden voyage of our homemade go-cart, which, by the way, was comprised of a lawnmower engine, Elmer's glue, and some two-by-fours, was certainly memorable. My dad decided he should be the one to test drive it first before putting the safety of his children on the line. I think he was just too excited to let any of us have the bragging rights. When he climbed upon the sawed-off wooden school chair, pulled the starter cord, and let that baby rip, the whole neighborhood took note. Maybe even the whole town. He took off like a rocket so loud that the cops came

30

within minutes. By then the chair had shaken loose and the brakes given out. I know what you're thinking: didn't they learn anything from the go-cart debacle? Don't they know that sometimes the term "DIY" stands for the "Dummy In Youth?" But this idea of do-it-yourself was so deeply engrained it was impossible to think otherwise.

After the lawnmower fiasco my mom convinced dad that buying a "brand new" used trampoline from the Salvation Army would somehow be safer than us breaking our necks on a homemade version. So we tied it to the roof of our station wagon, dragged it home, and set it up in the backyard. Now this wasn't just a second-hand trampoline. It looked as if it might have been the first trampoline ever made! The prototype. A "museum quality" trampoline, as my dad would say. (Same era as the trumpet I had to play in marching band). In my father's vernacular, anything old enough to be barely functioning earned the distinction of being "museum quality."

It was up to us kids to give this trampoline a little zing. We tightened the springs and lubed them up with some WD-40. I didn't tell anyone but I also rubbed some into a rag and wiped down the mat with it for added slickness. In no time we were doing flips, splits, and triple swivel hips. But for my brother it was

strictly about height. The higher the better and nothing would stop him.

The first week he could jump up to the branch our tree swing was tied to. Next, to the height of the bus we rode to school. But he wouldn't be happy until he could reach the attic window. We masterminded a plan where he would plunge off the roof of the garage dead center on the tramp. The height of the drop combined with the extra bounce he got from his Air Jordans would give him that much-needed edge.

It was the day of his record-setting jump and everything seemed to be going according to plan. I would be the spotter and was ready for anything. He leapt off the roof, went sailing through the air, and hit his mark right in the sweet spot. Except upon landing, his left leg also tore right through the trampoline canvas at the same time that the frame collapsed in on itself.

That was pretty much the end of that contraption.

My brother likes to say he was like Icarus flying too close to the sun and burning his wings. I think he was just getting greedy.

5

Cold Comfort

Every family has its rituals: decorate the house for the holidays, tick off the kids' inches on the door frame, chill your pillows on a hot night in the refrigerator before bed.... *What?!* It seemed like a brilliant invention laying your weary little head on a cool, crisp, fluffy pillow. Sent us right off to dreamland. God forbid my parents would spring for an air conditioner.

All this seemed normal, but then so did a mom that short-sheeted our beds just for kicks. I also thought everyone's grandmother was called Gaga. (As in,

"I wish I could hang out with you guys on Saturday, but I have to go see my Gaga.") Perhaps the most embarrassing moment of sixth grade.

We chilled our pillows long into September and when the warm winds of spring drifted in the next year, we couldn't wait to get those pillows on ice. As it got hotter and hotter on the plains of our Midwest home, it was no longer enough to feel the coolness on our cheeks: we needed it all the way down to our toes.

We started putting everything in the fridge—pillows in the freezer, sheets in the crisper, PJs rolled up in the butter compartment, we even put in baseball mitts and T-shirts—leaving all the food to spoil on the kitchen counter. Let me tell you, it was well worth the sacrifice.

We ate toast without margarine, P.B.'s without the J., and cereal without the milk. My parents' rule of "no sugar cereal" soon became lax and brands like Honeycomb passed simply by using the argument quoted on the box: "It's a delicious part of a nutritious breakfast." Cap'n Crunch—a tougher sell to be sure—would not be far behind. All that begging for "store-bought" cookies like Oreo and Chips Ahoy was now paying off big time. Preservatives were our friends. Dinners now consisted exclusively of things that came in vacuum-sealed pouches and could be microwaved so that the outside elicited third-degree burns while the inside remained partially frozen. But, no more meatloaf! No fish sticks, no eggs, no more crummy homemade stuff. We could live in junk-food bliss like the other kids in our neighborhood.

Then one rueful day, dad, all smiles, brought home a big, giant air conditioner, and 10,000 BTUs later, life got a lot less interesting.

6

Bundle of Joy

I was a junior in high school when out of the blue one day my parents call my brother and me into the living room for a family meeting. We sat nervously on the scratchy, plaid sofa awaiting the news. What could it be?

I had a hunch that told me we were moving. Definitely moving.

Well, I'm not going, I argued in my head. I'll live with Mary Melling's family until I finish high school. And that's that.

Maybe my brother and I could get after-school jobs and share an apartment in town. Walk to school. Take care of each other.

My father did all the talking. "Well, kids, your mother and I have something to tell you…"

Here it comes.
We're definitely not going. No matter what.

"Your mother is pregnant." My dad continued to talk, but all I heard was blah, blah, blah. Like how parents sound in those Charlie Brown TV specials. I was still trying to digest his first statement.

What? I can't comprehend what you're saying, dad?!! That is impossible. How could this happen… gross! No way! What about us? That baby's going to monopolize your attention from now on and we'll be stuck taking care of the little monster whenever mom has errands to run. We'll be indentured babysitters.

"This is not good news," my brother whispered.

Then I had what some people might call a white light experience. A switch flipped and suddenly I had an entirely different take on the announcement: with an infant distracting them, wouldn't they be too busy to notice our transgressions and too tired to make a fuss if we were out past curfew? If our grades weren't perfect? If our chores weren't done?

But when the little guy returned from the hospital with mom, none of the mischievous thoughts

44

mattered anymore. He was cute and defenseless and we all pitched in to help however we could. I tried to think of ways to make life easier for my mom and came up with this list of inventions (patents pending).

1. The hands-free baby feeder, based on those beer-can hats you see at football games
2. A baby shoehorn
3. Disposable diapers printed to look like denim jeans
4. A soundproof crib
5. A bouncing highchair baby burper
6. A onesie baby mop to help with housework
7. A baby-stroller with built-in sound system
8. An inflatable wall to keep the baby out of my important, private, grown-up stuff
9. Baby self-tanner (because they can't lay out with their sensitive skin)

"Baby self-tanner? That doesn't help mom at all," my brother said emphatically.

"But everyone looks better with some color," I rebutted. "And boy, he is pale."

"That's just weird."

7

As Fabric Would Have It

In the world of elementary school education, swank cocktail parties are hardly the norm. PTA Night is about the closest they get to black tie, so when the first man to walk on the moon came to our town, it was the biggest thing to happen to us since the Broncos won the State Finals. Mister Neil Armstrong was to speak at the school assembly with a reception to immediately follow at the Golden Pines County Club. Neither my mom nor my dad had ever been there. My dad dusted off the same suit he'd worn to every wedding, funeral, and baptism for the last twenty years, but my mom insisted on making something special.

She paid a visit to Finn's Fabrics, picked out a few yards of an elaborate gold brocade, and got a Simplicity home sewing pattern. She had less than a week to put it all together. I remember her cutting it out on the living room floor, tracing around her body like a crime scene victim to get the fit just right. I helped her stitch it together after school, creating a perfect Jackie Onassis meets Marlo Thomas cocktail gown.

The big day arrived and mom went to the beauty shop to have her hair done up while Mr. Armstrong talked to us kids at the school auditorium. He talked about space travel and how anything was possible if you put your mind to it.

The reception afterward was for adults only; however, I insisted my parents take along a camera so I would have a memento. The country club made all the waiters wear tuxedos and most of the women arrived in fur stoles even though it was like 70 degrees outside. My parents valet-parked and made their grand entrance.

Dad saddled straight up to the bar and ordered his favorite drink, an Old Fashioned, while mom did the polite thing and headed for the receiving line. When

Neil Armstrong complimented her on the dress she'd made, Mom was over the moon!

The place was packed and buzzing with excitement. My parents mingled a bit and then went looking for a seat (Mom didn't find herself in heels too often and needed a break).

As they rounded the corner into the library, they were shocked to see that every club chair in the room was upholstered in the exact same fabric as Mom's gown. My dad quickly tried throwing his sportcoat over her the way someone might throw a blanket over a person who's unexpectedly caught fire.

I don't know if humiliation was what she was feeling at that moment, but rather than fight it, Mom made the best out of the situation. Isn't it always better to make like you were in on the joke? I think so.

To this day, the only picture we have of the astronaut's visit to our town is a photograph of my mom sitting in one of those chairs. All that you see —since her body is blending in with the fabric—is her head and her arms as if they were somehow floating in space.

Luxury Camping

Every July my family packed up the car and took to the open road, the back of the station wagon crammed with coolers, lanterns, a propane stove, canned goods, sleeping bags, and an inflatable air mattress. Mom was the co-pilot armed with too many maps, a Triple A card and the Kampgrounds of America directory. She plotted our cross-country journey with military precision. Each morning we would have breakfast at the campsite, then fold up the tent, and cover 200 miles before lunch—preferably with a tourist point of

interest in between: places like Pioneertown and Teepee Village, where suburban families could all have jobs re-creating life as early settlers. I also remember President James Garfield's historic birthplace in Cuyahoga County, Ohio.

"Can't you guys just drop me off at the Great Lakes Mall?"

Then back in the car for another six hours.

"Can we all make it an extra 30 miles for a campground with a pool?"

"Are there flush-toilets?"

"Sweet!"

The swankiest chain of campgrounds was called KOA. Anytime they spelled a word like "Kozy Kitchen" or "Kampground of America" you knew it would be good—like adding the "pe" on the end of shoppe to make it sound more old-world.

While my brother frittered the day away in the car drawing pictures of little men shooting monsters, I imagined the kind of camping vacation I would take if I had my druthers. The back seat of the station wagon would be my private salon. Lime green (my favorite color that year) shirred drapes and pillows would create my *I Dream of Jeannie* sanctuary.

"Natural Beauty"

And we'd eat lunch only at restaurants with cloth napkins. I'd had enough bologna and cheese singles sandwiches to last a lifetime.

Why couldn't camping be just a touch more luxurious? Given a few more flashlights, I could fashion them into a chandelier. Tibetan carpets layered jauntily inside the tents would be so much more comfortable. Why didn't Louis XIV ever make a camp stool? And if the tent was made of canvas, why not paint something artistic on the walls? A mural in the wilderness.

The decor was just the beginning. More importantly, my fashion sense had to survive in the great outdoors. High-heeled hiking boots, a purple velvet rucksack, and a glittery satin down vest sounded good to me. All these campers looked so "earthy." How about a little glamour, people?! I used charcoal for eyeliner and stained my lips with berries a fierce red, like some dark and mysterious forest nymph. I topped all this off with a twig hairdo and matchstick necklaces.

Smokey the Bear beware.

9

Bottling the Ball

My grandmother used to tell us fantastical bedtime stories. This one, about the Duchess, was my favorite.

~

The parties were legendary at this point, ever since her signature drink, Bride's Blush, had become all the rage from Bristol to Baton Rouge. When a bidding war broke out among Paris' perfumers as to which house would create The Duchess' scent, she decided it should be something festive and so Monsieur Nez was dispatched to Garland Castle with the task of bottling her annual Floriental Ball.

The hillsides were surrounded by groves of oranges, fields of lavender, tuberose, and jasmine, with umbrella pines lining the lane. He scurried about collecting the quintessence of each in specimen jars he then kept in a leather doctor's bag.

Over the driveway, her groundskeeper con-structed a lattice canopy of cedar where pink honey-suckle grew wilder by the season. Time-release seduction was her weapon of choice, manifesting itself in her approach to entertaining and the belief that a party should mature as the evening progressed. To that end, the Duchess staggered her invitations like an orchestra building to a crescendo.

Flourishes of sounds echoed throughout the mirrored ballroom, as the first of her guests arrived, butlers splitting sandalwood behind the stables to feed the fires, a dozen babies being tickled in an upstairs bedroom, the chaos competing for your sensory detec-tion.

It was a finely tuned craziness the Duchess sought to unleash. Quite at odds with traditional ball-throw-ing, she wanted your attention constantly under attack, never a moment to collect one's thoughts until you were tossed back in your carriage for the bumpy ride home.

The Duchess

Mademoiselle Candy Apple   *The Earl of Pommade*

Monsieur Nez

Even before they had served the mint stew, Monsieur Nez found he'd run out of specimen jars and surrendered to note-taking for the remainder of the night. The Duchess would have none of it and despite his better judgment she pushed him to comingle his samples in already occupied vessels. So cherry smoke from the Earl of Pommade's pipe was bottled along with powder from the rouge of Mademoiselle Candy Apple. In all, he collected close to three hundred samples from her dance, but ultimately it wasn't a matter of what you distilled, but the portion of the evening you wished to capture. You would never see the entirety of the celebration, but you could taste the ball in the back of your throat. The party lived on the tip of your tongue.

10

Serendipity on the El Train

In Chicago they call the subway system the El train because rather than being subterranean, most of the tracks are elevated above the city's traffic.

I took great pride in my ability to traverse the city from end to end, east to west, north to south without ever peeking at a map. I knew every station and it was at one of those stops, oddly enough, that my career began.

On my way to the Art Institute one morning I happened to be wearing a little number that I'd recently whipped up on my sewing machine. I admit

I was looking quite smart for an average school day. So, while I was waiting for the train, a woman approached me and asked me about the jacket I was wearing.

"Cute, whose is it?"
"Oh, mine! I'm a designer."
"Really? Well, here's my card. I'm the buyer for the fanciest store in all of Chicago. Be in my office Monday at 10:00 a.m. with your collection."

72 hours later...

I had sewn all weekend: a capsule collection consisting of three dresses, a tricked-out velveteen jacket, and a two-piece shirt-jacket and cropped-pant matching ensemble. Sunday night I packed them all in one of those black plastic garment bags borrowed from my boyfriend's interview suit.

Her office was slightly less impressive than I expected for someone of such high style status. I had imagined stepping into an atelier in the tradition of Coco Chanel, not Charles Schwab. We got down to business, and I went through my bag of goodies. While showing her the five styles I took on a little game show hostess/magician's assistant aplomb, making slow-motion hand sweeps over every item I presented. I really didn't have a clue what I was supposed to be doing anyway.

She sat at her desk with pen in hand studying each piece.

"What's the style number on that one?"

"Um…one."

"Really? OK. And the style number on *that?*"

"Two."

I was quickly blowing my novice cover.

"Well, then let me guess…three, four, and five?"

"Exactly!"

"Have you ever done this before?"

"Oh, sure. I sell to a bunch of smaller, you know, very exclusive boutiques. Mostly in Europe. You probably wouldn't know…."

"I'll need your vendor number."

"My…vendor number." *Think fast.* "Hmm… I'll have to, um, get back to you on that. My assistant can, ah…OK, I confess! I've never done this before, but if you give me the order I promise to deliver on time and make sure everything is perfect. And I'll be indebted to you for the rest of my life!"

She wrote the order for a dozen pieces of the velveteen jacket. I cut every piece on the floor in my apartment and sewed each one on my Singer sewing machine. In the end, the way I figured it, if you divided the time I spent making the stuff by the wholesale price, I was just about clearing minimum wage. Passion has no price. I delivered them ASAP to her office two weeks later in a Saks shopping bag (note to fledgling designers: don't ship merchandise to a client in their competitor's shopping bags).

"Hi, here's your stuff!"

"What are you doing here? Didn't you read the back of the purchase order? You ship to the warehouse…Okay, just leave them here."

The jackets sold in record time and I got a check in the mail.

Next stop, New York City.

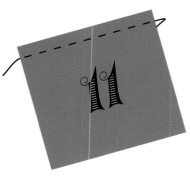

11

Laura of Arabia

M y cousin Laura and I needed a vacation, but couldn't agree on where to
go. We took turns spinning the globe
and I closed my eyes and pointed.
Destination: Northern Africa. We had always fantasized about the desert, but only knew it secondhand
from Humphrey Bogart movies and Paul Bowles
novels.

The day after we landed in Casablanca five German tourists were killed near the Libyan border and yet we remained undeterred—the romance of it all blinding us from the ruthless truth. We rented a car and drove south. Marrakech was the first stop and our last brush with civilization. We sprung for one night at the famous La Mamounia where Laura drew a bath and filled it with rose petals just like in the movies. The last thing I did before we checked out was swipe the bed sheet – the sheet that would later save our lives.

The Sahara was calling. "Laura of Arabia." We drove our beat-up Subaru straight south, past the Atlas Mountains into the dry, flat desert. After a couple of days, we ran out of road and were just driving aimlessly when we met a very friendly Berber family. They invited us into their heavy, black wool tent for tea. Laura speaks French and most Moroccans speak French or Arabic, so we enjoyed quite a chatty little tea party. They suggested we take along Uncle Mussad to help navigate and we could just leave him when the sand got too deep to drive. Were we suspicious? Not a bit! Until we saw his four missing fingers. A thief!

The rental car only made it another few miles until we were at the foothills of the dunes. We ditched Uncle Mussad and hired a couple of camels and two teenage Bedouins to guide us in the Sahara. *Fodors* may

have been a better option.

We rode for about eight hours under the blazing sun and they walked. They waxed poetically about the oasis where we would spend the night. We imagined a tropical paradise where palm trees swayed and piña coladas flowed under a perfect full moon.

Instead, we found a little muddy hole next to a scrubby, parched bush.

"Voilà, mademoiselles!"

"Voilà?"

"Non piscine?"

"Non garçons avec les boissons?"

"Non jus de pamplemousse?"

We slid the blankets off the camels' backs and, at the suggestion of our guides, dragged them high up on the dune so that the small animals wouldn't get us. What were these nasty little beasts? Worse yet, we were in the middle of absolutely nowhere with two strange men. Even if we screamed at the top of our lungs there wasn't a soul for miles who would ever hear us. Our only hope

for survival: we would have to take turns sleeping. Two hour shifts. The sky was pitch black with the brightest stars I've ever seen. About a minute later, we were both out cold. During the night a vicious sandstorm whipped over our camp and we were nearly buried alive. The only thing that shielded us from the storm and spared us from death? Our "borrowed" sheet.

12

Radically Clad Plaid Dad

The science of plaid:

Which came first, the tartan or the check?
Survival of the plaidest
For everything plaid there is an
    equal and opposite plaid
Plaid in motion will remain in motion
The atomic number of plaid is?

My dad has always fancied himself as a bit of
an outlaw, the kind of renegade who doesn't follow

convention, and his choice of clothing was no exception. "You know, Cynthia, I'm going to hold on to these six-inch-wide plaid ties, because they'll be back someday. And I'll be ready for it."

Let's hope not.

So when Chuck Hines, the finest menswear emporium in Neighborville, Illinois, cleaned out its inventory, the first thing to go was the stock of fine polyester plaid pants. To trend watchers this may have signaled the end of a look. To my dad, this meant an entire wardrobe upgrade. Fifteen pairs in the jackpot—and with only one duplicate! A two-week cycle with a spare. Life was good.

My mother refused to hem them—her subtle way of saying she didn't want him in public. So, he hemmed them himself.

Being in sort of a New Wave phase myself, I found the different-length pant legs kind of radical. This was total fashion confidence—and why not add different-colored socks? What did a striped shirt say worn with a hooded sweatshirt zipped-up and tied tightly around the face? Mystery! Now, throw in a pair of earmuffs under the hood, worn faithfully between the months of September through March. And who says plaids can't be mixed? *(Drop me off here, Dad. I'll walk the rest of the way to school.)*

Later, much later, in life, I started to appreciate my father's sartorial hubris, even his self-confidence, even his eccentricity. Ironically, this was around the same time you start to realize similarities in yourself. "Maybe that's cool? You know, he's his own man."

As a fashion designer, I found the whole thing inspiring, so I asked him to be in one of my runway shows. I called from New York and, while at first he wasn't sure, I called back three hours later and my mom said he couldn't come to the phone because he was watching fashion television and practicing his walk. He ended up coming to New York, doing the show, and the next day the *New York Post* ran a picture of him wearing all plaid, calling him the best model on any catwalk, EVER! He told me it was the happiest day of his life. My mom reminded him, "What about our wedding day? The birth of your three children? The day the White Sox won the World Series?" Nope, the happiest day. Now he's going by one name, Eddie, and telling everyone he has a go-see with Calvin.

I told my dad that if I see him on the side of a bus in his underwear I'm going to have to leave town.

SeaWorld

When Sea World calls, people listen. After all, it's not every day a designer gets a break of this magnitude. Apparently the folks at Disney, with their puffed-up, over-the-top fancy-pants costumes were starting to give the critters at Sea World an inferiority complex. Morale

93

was running on fumes and the powers that be thought it was time for a makeover.

That's where I came in.

"Complete image overhaul…Cirque du Soleil with scales…gills on parade…."

I was intrigued.

Most of these fish hadn't changed their look in eons. I mean, you can't let evolution do all the work for you. So where to begin? First on the agenda: dressing down the penguins, moving some casual pieces into their wardrobe. Give them jeans and a hoodie. Catapult these guys into the twenty-first century.

Next up, I called in a favor from my connection on 47th Street and had gold grills made up for all the sharks. The whales and dolphins got fitted for giant headdresses so that when their blowholes exploded, streamers would shoot high into the air. The catchword here was "volume." The parrotfish were already looking very Versace, so a smattering of Swarovski crystals took it up just that one extra notch. The eels demanded something strapless and slinky, which I was happy to oblige.

Now the stingrays really needed to soften their image, put some spin on their species. I thought "floral" and "flirty." Something that says, "I'm approachable. No, I won't stab you in the heart when you're not looking."

I went full gangster with the shrimp costumes and worked up a number to the tune, "It's Hard Out Here for a Shrimp."

I worked round the clock passionately combining breathtaking fabrics, brilliant trims, and bewitching shapes to redefine marine life as we know it. Their next show opened to rave reviews and photos splashed across the newspaper with headlines like "Atlantis Found!" It was a proud moment for sea life everywhere and perhaps my greatest work to date. Or maybe I'm just fishing for compliments.

14

On With the Show

I've always thought a fashion show should be a SHOW!

I like to start with a theme. It gives me a foundation to work from, a thread for inspiration. The clothes are most important but I like to carry the theme all the way through to the invitations, the music, the venue, and even a little something extra *during* the show. A few times, I admit, I may have gone too far.

One of my earliest shows was based on a pirate theme (think cover of a romance novel). It was held on one of those sightseeing tour boats. The waiters wore eye patches and puffy shirts and got as sloppy drunk as Captain Hook and his men. (My belief is if you're inviting guests you should serve them some sort of food and beverage.) The models were instructed to walk down the aisles showing off the collection. But with the choppy conditions and high winds, the models wavered and fell into people's laps until most were just too seasick to go on. My captive audience was trapped for three hours at sea and talk of *Gilligan's Island* and *Mutiny on the Bounty* abound. But it didn't dampen my spirit for more fashion adventure.

One season, I blew up the runway—literally. The lights went out and the gunpowder fuse sizzled 100 feet down the middle of the catwalk, exploding at the end as the first model came out in a cute little pink dress with the entire bottom singed.

Danger is always a good way to keep the audience on the edge of their folding chairs. Pushing fashion forward is about kicking down doors. Or in the case of my last spring show—kicking through a

wall of frosted glass. We used the same material that stunt men use in movies—"candy glass"—like when a cowboy gets thrown through the window of a saloon. So I assured the first model that it would be perfectly safe to smash her stiletto through it and then stomp over the broken glass that got sprayed all over the place. It was only later when I watched the video that I noticed a trickle of blood running down the back of this girl's leg. She took it like a champ and I sent her a dozen roses and some Band-Aids the next day. Only a few seat-belt-wearing goody-two-shoes were really shocked.

Sometimes proper etiquette can be shocking in its own way. There was the dinner party show, where the runway was raised and was set with formal place settings positioned just far enough apart for the girls to saunter past them as if they had jumped onto the banquet table to show off their outfits. It ended with a parade of party dresses topped off with jaunty teacup hats, coffee, tea…

When I happened upon the idea to have a show in the ballroom of the New Yorker Hotel, how could I not kick it off with the tristate champion waltzers? This duo had tangoed and foxtrotted their way to the top of every dance competition since the mid-seventies. So when they had the chance to show off in front of all those movers and shakers…there was no way they were going to be cut short! In fact, they wouldn't stop! It seemed like hours! The fashion crowd has no patience for that kind of thing. "Get the hook," we yelled from backstage. But they just kept going

and going
and going.

That should have been a red flag. But that wasn't all I had up my sleeve.

The show ended with the lights going down and all the girls coming out wearing dresses with tiny lights placed in between layers of fabric. Each dress had its very own battery pack, except the batteries somehow dislodged from the dresses and were swinging between the girls' legs, short-circuiting the lights and tripping up the models. Not so sexy.

The smart money would have given up some variety at that point if the trade-off was peace of mind, but not me.

Months later, it was show time again and what a better venue for a hot summer men's show than a penthouse swimming pool? We decided to open with synchronized swimmers. I'm thinking buff girls in black tank suits with gold caps.

Slam dunk.

Then the swim team arrived that day looking more like members of my mom's aquasize class. But the crowd loved them anyhow. The guys were perfect and the show went off without a hitch. It was time for the roundup finale where all the male models come out in their last look and I come out for a thank-you wave to the crowd for all their support.

Watching the show later, I could see where it all got away from me.

Coming around the home stretch of the final lap, you can see one guy sort of twitch and then dive into the pool. Within seconds, every model was diving and splashing in the pool. My entire collection—leather pants, tailored jackets, shoes, and belts—was floating in the pool. Of course I had to dive in and join them.

Music can change the whole mood of the show. All of a sudden something that is meant to look Moroccan can be transformed into a parade of the Ballets Russes if the music isn't right. So when I worked with my artist friend Will Cotton to transform our show into Candyland, the music had to be perfect without being too sugary sweet.

The show was held outside and as the threat of Hurricane Isabelle blew Hershey's Kiss wrappers

across the runway, under a black sky, my friend Scarlett Johansson belted out her own version of "The Candy Man." And when she asked, "Who can make the sun shine?" We all agreed....

Acknowledgments

Very special thanks to Charles Miers at Rizzoli who inspired this collection of tall tales. I came to him with a half-baked idea and he turned it into a pear frangipane tarte.

And everyone else at Rizzoli who encouraged and supported the publication of this book. Ellen Nidy, Ellen Cohen, and Maria Pia Gramaglia.

Art director Willy Wong who lent his talent and (patience) to this project.

And my bright and imaginative staff especially Jessica Farrugia, William Eadon, Rachel Konikiewicz, and Michelle Finocchi.

Published by Rizzoli International Publications, Inc.
300 Park Avenue South
New York, NY 10010
www.rizzoliusa.com

Copyright © 2007 Cynthia Rowley

2007 2008 2009 2010 2011 / 10 9 8 7 6 5 4 3 2 1

All illustrations and text are by Cynthia Rowley
Rizzoli Editor: Ellen Cohen
Design by Willy Wong

ISBN: 0-8478-2923-5
ISBN-13: 978-0-8478-2923-1
Library of Congress
Catalogue Number: 2007920068

Printed in Italy